Ethereum Investing 2022

The Best Guide to Understanding Ethereum, Blockchain, Smart Contracts, ICOs, and Decentralized Apps.

Table of Contents

Introduction to Ethereum

"When I came up with Ethereum, my first thought was, okay this thing is too good to be true. As it turned out, the core Ethereum idea was good, fundamentally, completely, sound." - Vitalik Buterin, Creator of Ethereum

When Bitcoin was created in 2009, it was originally dismissed by many as just a way for criminals and computer experts to transfer fake internet money to each other. In less than 8 years, it has gone from being considered a scam to being seen as a technology that could disrupt finance, banks, foreign exchange and potentially create a worldwide global currency.

The change in perception is largely in part due to the realization of the potential of the blockchain technology underlying Bitcoin. Blockchain technology is more revolutionary than Bitcoin, and is predicted by many to have an impact on the world as big as the internet once did.

While many people have heard of Bitcoin, it is the lesser known Ethereum that made the world aware of the potential of blockchain technology. Bitcoin mainly used blockchain technology for payments and transfers of digital currency.

The creation of Ethereum has taken the possibilities of blockchain from a technology mainly used for financial payments into a technology that could disrupt and replace systems or companies in almost every industry in the world.

The original blockchain technology created by Bitcoin is known as Blockchain 1.0. The new capabilities that Ethereum has made blockchain technology capable of is known as blockchain 2.0

Ethereum is considered by many governments and corporations to be a far superior technology compared to Bitcoin. Large companies such as Microsoft, MasterCard, UBS, ING, Intel, BP, Deloitte, J.P Morgan and more have joined an alliance to work together on developing, building and integrating Ethereum based applications on a large scale.

Ethereum is not just an idea that may have an impact in the future. The

Ethereum platform has already shown to have a wide range of real world applications across a variety of industries.

Ethereum was only released in 2015, however in the short time it has been around, there have been thousands of companies and applications all created on the back of Ethereum.

Billions of dollars have been created in a few years as companies and developers utilize the revolutionary capabilities of Ethereum. Everything from digital identities, file sharing, cloud storage to chat messaging apps have already been created on Ethereum.

Ethereum is still a new technology, however it is one that is already set to change the world. Understanding Ethereum in these early stages, could put you in the cutting edge of a technology that may one day be a part of everyday life.

Even if you have had no experience with Bitcoin, Ethereum or cryptocurrencies, by the end of this book, you should have a firm understanding of what Ethereum is, how it works, and why it is so revolutionary.

Let us get started with the first chapter to understand exactly what Ethereum is.

Chapter 1: What Is Ethereum?

To understand Ethereum, it first helps to understand a bit about Bitcoin and decentralization.

Centralization Explained

Almost every website you access, application you use and financial transaction you make has a centralized company or institution involved.

When you upload a photo to Instagram, the app connects to the centralized Instagram servers. The photo is then sent to the servers where it is stored.

When another person opens the Instagram app, they connect to Instagram's centralized servers and access the photo directly from there.

Most of the time, centralized applications like Instagram work fine for the majority of people. However, they do have significant downsides and risks.

Centralized servers are prone to hacking. If someone manages to hack a centralized server like Instagram, they could potentially obtain user details, photos and messages. If a centralized server is attacked or there is a server issue, then the server and applications may be unavailable for all users.

Centralized websites, applications and servers can also be blocked by governments. China has blocked a lot of major websites such as Google, Facebook, Twitter and YouTube, along with any websites that don't comply with the Chinese government's rules on censorship and sharing data about their users with the government.

Hacking, censorship and server downtime are common risks associated with centralized servers and applications.

Decentralization Explained

With regards to Ethereum, decentralization distributes the servers and computing power across a network of computers. These computers are all connected and work together like one large supercomputer. However, each computer also operates independently and the network doesn't rely on every computer to operate.

If one server goes offline, then the other servers will still operate without issue. The benefits of running a decentralized system of multiple servers was explained simply by Vitalik Buterin, when he stated that it is much more likely that one computer server will fail than for five out of ten servers to fail at the same time.

In a decentralized system, in order for a hacker to access the system, they would need to gain access to the majority of computers on the network at the same time. While each computer operates separately, they work together as one single supercomputer. The entire supercomputer can't be controlled unless the majority of computers are controlled at the same time.

There are thousands of computers on the Ethereum network, so in order for the system to be hacked, thousands of computers would have to be hacked at the same time, which is almost impossible.

Later in the book, we'll go into more detail about exactly how the decentralization of the Ethereum network works.

Bitcoin's Decentralized Network

Bitcoin has a decentralized network of computers all working together. Bitcoin has more computers than Ethereum and the network has been around for longer. The computing power of the Bitcoin network is greater than the 500 most powerful supercomputers combined.

It would seem that Bitcoin has all the advantages of a decentralized network of computers that Ethereum has, so why is Ethereum seen as superior to Bitcoin?

The computers connected to the Bitcoin network process financial transactions and can perform a few limited tasks. While the Bitcoin network has immense computing power, most of this computing power is directed towards validating and adding transactions to the Bitcoin ledger. The Bitcoin network is not capable of running complex applications or utilising the computing power for other purposes.

Ethereum Virtual Machine

The Ethereum network has the Ethereum Virtual Machine, which can run computer programs.

Previously, when a developer wanted to write a computer program, they would write it in the standard computing programming languages and would run it on a centralized server or computer.

The blockchain technology underlying Bitcoin offers a lot of potential; however, in order to utilise blockchain technology, developers have to create their own blockchain along with a network of computers to run it.

Building a distributed network of people willing to contribute computing power and resources to a new blockchain is complicated, especially with the large number of blockchain-based systems being created each week.

Creating any meaningful application on blockchain technology required significant costs, resources and time. This was not possible for most people or companies to create.

The Ethereum Virtual Machine allows developers to run computer programs on a blockchain. The computer programs can be written in a code that is similar to common programming languages developers already use. Ethereum also has an existing network of computers connected together ready to run applications.

The Ethereum Supercomputer

One of the reasons Ethereum is so powerful is that computer programmers can create applications in programming languages they already know. They can run these programs on a powerful supercomputer made up of a decentralized network of computers.

Applications running on the decentralized network of computers are much less likely to go offline or be hacked. The computing power of the network of computers is also far more powerful than individual centralized servers or computers.

With Ethereum, developers and companies can utilise blockchain technology in their applications without having to create their own blockchain or build a network of computers to run it.

End of Chapter Notes on Ethereum

You should now have an idea of what Ethereum is. In the next chapters, we'll cover how Ethereum and blockchain technology works, along with decentralized applications and smart contracts.

Chapter 2: Understanding Blockchain technology

Blockchain technology is one of the key foundation technologies of Ethereum. In this chapter, we'll cover exactly what blockchain technology is and how it works.

What is the blockchain?

The first blockchain was created with Bitcoin, the source code of Bitcoin includes notes that describe groups of transactions as blocks connected together like a chain.

With Bitcoin, financial transactions are grouped together into a "block" of transactions. The blocks of transactions act like a digital ledger of all the transactions that have occurred on the Bitcoin network.

Every 10 minutes, a new block of transactions is added to the existing blocks. Each block has a unique number, which increases with each new block. The first block on the blockchain is "block 0," the next block after that is "block 1," followed by "block 2" and so on. When a new block is added, it is connected to the previous block by referring to it within the block data.

Block 100 includes a reference to block 99 as the previous block.
Block 99 includes a reference to the block 98 as the previous block.
This continues all the way to the first block on the blockchain, which is block 0.

The data in the block is unique, even the smallest change such as changing a letter from lowercase to uppercase will alter the block details. If the block details are changed, it breaks the chain. In order to hack a blockchain and manipulate transactions, every block after the altered block would need to be changed as well. This is almost impossible after an hour on many blockchains as too many blocks will have been added.

Decentralized blockchain

With existing centralized systems, a third party or central authority manages transactions. When you transfer money from one bank account to a bank account with another bank, each bank has their own centralized ledgers, checks, and processes. The first bank checks to see that you have sufficient money in the account and are authorized to transfer the money. If all the checks are correct and valid, they send the money to the other bank. The receiving bank then checks the bank account details are correct and reconciles the money received on their ledgers before depositing it in the account.

Most blockchains such as Ethereum are decentralized. With a decentralized blockchain, all transactions are reconciled and processed on the same ledger. The checks and processes are conducted by the computers on the network. When a transfer is sent, it is checked by computers on the network as to whether the sender has sufficient funds and authorization to send the transaction. If the computers determine it is a valid transaction, the transaction is grouped into a block of transactions that are added to the blockchain.

The majority of computers on the network are checking each block of transactions added to the blockchain. There is no central authority required to process transactions. Banks don't process transactions when they are closed, or there are no staff are working. However, with a decentralized blockchain, transactions are processed by computers on the network 24 hours a day, 7 days a week.

Ethereum Blockchain

Before Ethereum, blockchain based systems were mainly created to contain financial transactions. There were very few practical applications of blockchain technology outside of cryptocurrencies or finance.

While the potential of blockchain technology was starting to be realized before Ethereum, every new idea required its own unique blockchain and network of computers.

In order to apply blockchain technology to a new idea, an entirely new blockchain would have to be created. This would require a cryptocurrency along with a network of computers contributing computing power to run the network.

The blockchain would then be specific to the purpose it was created for. A blockchain based system for financial transactions, couldn't also process transactions involving other types of data.

The Ethereum blockchain can contain contracts, computer code, and almost any type of data. Applications can be built that run on top of the Ethereum blockchain and utilize the existing computing power of the Ethereum network.

Blocks of data can't be altered or reversed, which is where the power of Ethereum can be seen across many industries. It is easy to create an application on the Ethereum blockchain, any data recorded on the blockchain will create a permanent record of that information.

Data in a block can't be altered or changed, any changes will be made in future blocks on the blockchains that are linked to the previous blocks. This creates a permanent record and an audit trail of all actions and changes that have occurred since the first entry on the blockchain.

There is no confusion as to what was originally agreed upon or the changes that have been made. Each change is timestamped and permanently recorded on the blockchain. This immutable audit trail can be applied to any application or contract.

End of Chapter Notes on Blockchain Technology

Blockchain technology is a revolutionary innovation created in the source code of Bitcoin and is one of the foundation technologies of Ethereum. It is similar to a database, where data, transactions, and records of value can be recorded.

Transactions are grouped into blocks and connected to the other blocks linking them together like a chain. This chain of blocks along with the transactions in the blocks can't be altered or deleted—thereby creating a permanent record of all transactions that have occurred.

Transactions on a blockchain-based system don't require an intermediary such as a bank or company to validate or process transactions. When you transfer money between bank accounts, the transaction is validated by the banks and their internal systems. A transaction on a blockchain-based system doesn't require a bank to validate the transaction, it is checked and validated by other computers on the network. If the majority of computers agree the transaction is valid, then it will be processed.

There is no centralized company or government that controls the blockchain, it doesn't rely on one central server or organization to operate.

Before Ethereum, most blockchains were used for financial transactions. Ethereum has made it possible for blockchain technology to be easily used to record anything of value in almost any industry in the world.

Chapter 3: History of Ethereum

To understand the history of Ethereum, it is first worth mentioning Bitcoin as it had been in existence for several years before Ethereum was created. Bitcoin created the first blockchain and a lot of the ideas and code behind Ethereum wouldn't have been possible if it weren't for Bitcoin.

The Creator of Ethereum

Vitalik Buterin is the inventor and co-creator of Ethereum. He was born in Russia in 1994, but moved to Canada with his parents in 2000.

At the age of 19, Vitalik wrote about Bitcoin for blogs and co-founded a website called "Bitcoin Magazine." Along with writing about Bitcoin, Vitalik wrote code for Bitcoin and other cryptocurrencies.

Writing about Bitcoin and developing code for cryptocurrencies made him aware of the limitations and flaws of Bitcoin and other cryptocurrencies.

Each new cryptocurrency required a new network of computers, new developers, code and hardware to operate. Cryptocurrencies all operated independently, without interacting or connecting.

In late 2013, Vitalik published a white paper about Ethereum. Vitalik wasn't sure how the white paper would be received by people. He thought that he may have missed an obvious error or that it wasn't possible. He is quoted as saying, *"When I came up with Ethereum, my first thought was, okay this thing is too good to be true… as it turned out, the core Ethereum idea was good, fundamentally, completely, sound."*

When asked about how Vitalik came up with the name, he replied that he discovered the name while looking at elements from science fiction online. He liked how it sounded along with the fact that it contained the word "Ether," which is a "hypothetical invisible medium that permeates the universe and allows light to travel."

In early 2014, Vitalik started work on Ethereum with Gavin Wood and Jeffrey Wilke. The Ethereum "Yellow Paper" was then published, outlining the technical details of how Ethereum would work.

Ethereum would take a lot of development work and money to create. A crowdfunding campaign was created to raise funds to build the Ethereum platform. They raised $18 million in just over a month in exchange for the Ether cryptocurrency once the platform was created.

After 18 months of development, Ethereum was released to the public in mid-2015.

The DAO

About a year after Ethereum was released, some computer programmers created smart contracts on the Ethereum platform known as "The DAO."

DAO is an acronym for decentralized autonomous organization. It operates similar to a company or organization structure, but all decisions are made by votes of the DAO token holders.

The DAO was designed to be similar to a hedge fund for decentralized apps on the Ethereum platform. Programmers could pitch their dApp ideas and members of the DAO would vote on whether to fund the dApps or not.

The DAO had a crowdfunding campaign which raised over 150 million dollars in less than a month. After the crowdfunding campaign ended, it held almost 15 percent of all Ether created.

The DAO Attack

Some people expressed security concerns about the DAO, in particular vulnerabilities surrounding withdrawals.

With the computer code, instructions are run in the order they are written. Code that is written at the bottom will only be run after all the code before it has run.

The withdrawal function in the DAO only updated the balance after the withdrawal had occurred. This makes sense, if it is written correctly, the code would run as below:

- User sends withdrawal request for $100 to the DAO
- Computer code checks whether the user has a balance of $100

- If the user has a balance of $100, then withdraw $100 to the user
- Remove $100 from the user's balance after the withdrawal

The problem with the code in the DAO is that attackers were able to send multiple withdrawal requests before the balance was updated.

Assuming you have only $100 in your bank account. This would be like going into a bank and asking a teller to withdraw $100 from your account. The teller would check whether you have a balance of $100 and then go to the vault to withdraw the money.

While the first teller is withdrawing the money from the vault, you go to the next teller and ask them to withdraw $100 from your account. The second teller checks your balance. As your balance hasn't been updated with the withdrawal yet, they go to the vault to withdraw $100 for you.

The first teller comes back gives you $100 and updates your balance to $0 as you have withdrawn all your money. The second teller then comes back and updates your balance to $0 as well. In both cases, they seem valid because when they checked, you had money in your account. The balance hadn't been updated.

Now you have $200 in cash, you go to the bank and deposit that $200. You then repeat the withdrawal process, requesting a withdrawal of $200 from the first teller and $200 from the second teller. This continues until you have withdrawn all of the money in the banks vault.

This is similar to what happened to the DAO. Deposits were made and then withdrawn multiple times until more than 50 million dollars was withdrawn from the DAO.

This attack on the DAO and error due to poorly written computer code is not a vulnerability in the Ethereum platform. The DAO is an application written on the Ethereum platform, just like a website running on the internet.

Gavin Wood, (the co-founder of Ethereum) states that claiming that Ethereum was hacked because the DAO was hacked is like saying the internet is broken when one website isn't working.

Chapter 4: Difference between Ethereum, Ethereum Classic and Bitcoin

By now, you should have a good understanding of what Ethereum is and how it works. In this chapter, we'll cover how Ethereum differs from Bitcoin and Ethereum Classic.

Bitcoin vs Ethereum

As covered earlier in the book, Ethereum has a computer platform and programming language that allows developers to create smart contracts and decentralized applications (dApps). Developers can utilise the computing power of a global decentralized network of computers on the Ethereum platform to run these dApps and smart contracts.

Bitcoin has a global decentralized network of computers; however, the computing power is mainly used for processing transactions. Bitcoin has no programming language or computing platform like Ethereum.

Bitcoin and Ethereum have their own blockchains for recording data. Bitcoin adds a new block to the Bitcoin blockchain approximately every 10 minutes. Ethereum adds a new block to the Ethereum blockchain approximately every 30 seconds.

Bitcoin's currency vs Ethereum's currency

Given the additional features that Ethereum has over Bitcoin, it may appear that Ethereum is superior and will replace Bitcoin as the dominant cryptocurrency.

However, Ethereum was not designed to be a replacement for Bitcoin. Ethereum and Bitcoin were designed for different reasons and are not competing against each other.

Bitcoin was the original cryptocurrency and blockchain network. The currency on the Bitcoin network, also called "bitcoin", was designed for financial transactions. Bitcoin is a global currency that exists outside the control of governments and financial institutions.

The currency of the Ethereum network, called "Ether", was designed to be used as payment for computing power on the Ethereum platform. When a developer wants to run an application on the Ethereum platform, they pay for the computing power using Ether.

Ether also exists outside the control of governments and financial institutions; however, it is designed to be a local currency used on the Ethereum platform.

Bitcoin has a fixed supply of 21 million bitcoins. This is to avoid devaluing the price of bitcoin by creating an excess supply. Ethereum has no limit on the number of Ether that can be created, meaning the price of Ether could decrease as supply continues to increase.

There are many websites and shops around the world that accept Bitcoin as a form of payment. As Bitcoin gains in popularity, it will be more accepted as a payment method alongside credit cards, PayPal, and cash. People can use bitcoins to pay for goods and services online or in stores.

Ether is not designed to be use in shops and websites as a form of payment. As Ethereum gains in popularity, it will be more accepted as a platform to develop applications on competing programming languages, operating systems, and computer servers. Developers and companies will buy Ether to use as payment for the computing power they use on the Ethereum network.

Ethereum vs Ethereum Classic

While Bitcoin and Ethereum were designed for different purposes, Ethereum and Ethereum Classic came from the same code and are similar to each other. There are major differences, which we'll cover in this section. The disagreement in the Ethereum community that led to the creation of the two Ethereum chains was covered earlier in the book.

Originally, there was only one Ethereum platform and currency; however, due to a code error in a smart contract, known as the DAO, the community split into two separate blockchains and currencies.

The DAO was one of the largest crowdfunded projects of all time. Over 150 million dollars of Ether was held by the DAO, which was 15% of the entire supply of Ether.

The code error in the smart contract was not a vulnerability or issue with

Ethereum. There was nothing wrong with the Ethereum platform; the smart contract had a flaw that was exploited, leading to 50 million dollars of Ether being stolen.

The error in the DAO smart contract was essentially like a contract that has a poorly worded clause, allowing one party to exploit the contract. If this happened with a contract, lawyers and courts would be brought in to argue this was not the intention of the clause.

With a smart contract, there are no lawyers or courts; the code of the contract is the law. The code was correct; however, it was badly written, like a badly worded legal contract.

The "hackers" stole 50 million dollars of Ethereum by exploiting this poorly worded piece of code. They didn't hack the system; they simply found a part of the code that allowed them to transfer the funds to themselves within the terms of the smart contract.

The Ethereum community voted the contract should be reversed, as this was not the intention of the code. Part of the community argued this was not a hack; the smart contract was valid. By reversing the transactions, the community is essentially acting like judges and courts deciding which contracts and transactions are valid.

By reversing the transactions, they would be acting like a third-party intermediary, deciding about changes to contracts running on the platform. This was against the original intention of the Ethereum platform, which should be decentralized, free from any government, company, or third-party interference. If the terms of a smart contract are valid, they should not be reversed; the code of the smart contract should be the law.

Due to the amount of funds stolen, the community voted to reverse the transactions, so everyone got their funds back. This is essentially like allowing one party involved in a contract to act as judge on whether the contract was valid. Many people voting had lost money, so they voted not necessarily on what was right, but because they wanted their money back.

To reverse the transactions, the blockchain was essentially reset to before the funds were stolen. This gained majority support, including the original creators of Ethereum.

Part of the community saw this decision as clearly violating the ideology and design of the Ethereum network, so they continued using the Ethereum platform and blockchain without reversing the transactions.

There were now two Ethereum blockchains and currencies being used, which created confusion. The original blockchain became known as Ethereum Classic and the currency as Ether Classic.

Ethereum classic was built on the principles of immutability, neutrality, decentralization, and the ideology that code is law. The community believes in developing the platform but remaining neutral to how the platform is used and not interfering with contracts or transactions on the network.

Ethereum classic has all the features and functionality of Ethereum; however, it has a much smaller community and less computing power supporting it. Currently, Ethereum classic is a similar but less supported version of Ethereum.

The current price of Ether is $300 USD, with a market capitalisation of $28 billion dollars. The current price of Ether classic is $15, with a total market capitalization of $1.5 billion dollars.

Ethereum classic aims to differentiate itself; however, it is uncertain whether it will gain the support to survive against Ethereum. The main Ethereum platform has significant support from developers, along with interest from government and large companies.

Chapter 5: Decentralized Apps (dApps)

By this point, you may be familiar with some of the differences between centralization and decentralization. In this chapter, we'll delve deeper into one of the major innovations introduced by Ethereum: decentralized apps running on a blockchain.

What are decentralized apps (dApps)?

Decentralized applications (dApps for short) are applications that, unlike traditional applications, have no central server. They run across a distributed network of computers and don't require a central server or company controlling them to work.

Users of dApps connect directly to each other instead of to a central server or company. While a company or software developer may create a dApp, once it is released it is controlled by the majority of users. The creator of the dApp can't censor or have central control over the app.

How dApps work

To better understand how dApps work, let's look at the difference between standard apps and dApps.

Difference between dApps and standard centralized apps:

Centralized apps:

Centralized apps are installed and run on a central server. When you access a website, you are accessing that website from the same server as everyone else. All data is sent from the central server to each user accessing it.

As mentioned earlier in the book, some of the risks of centralized applications are:

- Hacking: If the main server is hacked, all users' details could be vulnerable and hackers could control the application
- Server failure: If the main servers went offline, the entire application would go offline
- Censorship: Centralized websites, applications and servers can be blocked by governments

- Computing power: The more users connected to the server, the slower the server will be unless its computing power is continuously upgraded.

A dApp is not installed on a single central server but on multiple computers of users that contribute their computing power to the app.

If we look at how emails are currently sent using Gmail, we can compare the difference between centralized systems and dApps.

Currently when you send an email with Gmail, you log in to an application on your phone, computer or a website and connect to the central servers of Gmail. All your emails are stored and managed by the central server. The ability to send emails is handled by the server. When the email is sent, it is passed to the Gmail server that then sends it to the recipient.

If the Gmail server goes down, you are unable to send or receive emails. Your Internet connection may be working perfectly but because the server is not working, you can't access your emails. If the Gmail server is hacked, the hacker may gain access to all customer accounts and emails.

With a decentralized email app, you can contribute your computing power to the system and your computer will act like a server. When you access your emails, they are directly on your computer – you don't need to worry about connecting to a centralized server. When you send an email, it is sent directly from your computer to the recipient. It doesn't go through a third-party centralized server.

You don't have to contribute your computing power to the system – you can also just use the app. Other users will contribute their computing power, which acts like multiple servers all around the world. When you access your emails, you connect to one of these servers. Each server holds a copy of all the information in the app. If one of the servers goes down, you connect to another one and access your emails from there. Users connect directly to each other, without needing a third-party intermediary or centralized server to run the app or store the emails and data.

<u>Centralized file sharing</u>

You've probably used some form of centralized file sharing such as Google

Drive or Dropbox. Even downloading a file from a website is a form of centralized file sharing.

When sharing a file using a centralized server, the file is uploaded to one central server. All users downloading that file will download the same file from the same server. The more people downloading the file at the same time, the slower the server and download will become unless the server computing power is increased.

If the server is offline, the file will be unavailable and nobody will able to download it. If a government or the company that owns the server doesn't approve of the file being shared, they can block the file or server so the file can't be accessed.

If a hacker is able to hack the server, they could replace the file with a different version of the file that has a virus. Anyone attempting to download the file will then download the version of the file with the virus.

Decentralized file sharing

If you're old enough to remember Napster, or are familiar with a more recent file-sharing application like BitTorrent, then you are already familiar with decentralized file sharing.

With BitTorrent, every user has a copy of the application on their computer. They also store files on their computer they want to share.

When you search for a file on BitTorrent, it searches for all the users that have a copy of that file, and the results may show 100 people are sharing this file. When you choose to download that file, you are not connecting to or downloading it from a central server. Instead, you are connecting directly to all of the users' computers that have a copy of that file.

Each computer acts like a server with an exact copy of the file you want to download. If one of the servers goes offline, it doesn't impact your download because it just connects to another computer that is sharing that file and continues downloading from them.

If a lot of users are downloading the file at the same time, they will connect to the user with the file that has the fastest connection to them. They don't all connect to one centralized server, so a user from Europe may connect to another user from Europe sharing the file, while someone from the USA may connect to another user from the USA.

Once the users have downloaded the file, they can then select to share it as well so their computer becomes like a server. Other users can then connect directly to their computers to access and download the file. The more users that use BitTorrent and download files, the faster the file download times become as there are more servers sharing files.

If one of the computers sharing the file is hacked, the hacker doesn't get access to all the files or data on the network. They may be able to manipulate the files on that computer; however, with BitTorrent, in order for a file to be accepted as valid it has to be an exact copy of all the other files on the network.

If a hacker gets access to a computer and tries to put a virus on the files being shared, the files won't be an exact match of all the other files. When you attempt to download the same file, it may show 99 users sharing this file and one user sharing a different version of that file. As the majority of users agree that this is a valid file, most people downloading the file will trust the file that 99 users are sharing is valid and not the one different version of that file.

In order for a hacker to trick the system, they would have to hack the computers of the majority of users at the same time and put a virus in all of the files. Then, when a person tries to download the file, it would show that the majority of users are sharing that file. The person downloading the file may trust the majority of users are sharing the correct file and download the now-corrupted file with the virus.

If a government or company doesn't approve of the file being shared, they would have to block every person from sharing the file. As the people sharing the file are likely in different countries all around the world, it would be difficult to block them all unless the file is illegal in all the countries it is being shared.

dApps on the Ethereum platform

While BitTorrent is an easy-to-understand example of how decentralized systems can work, the app itself is not a dApp and it doesn't run on the Ethereum platform.

dApps on the Ethereum platform operate similarly to BitTorrent; however, there are some major differences.

Open source

dApps are open source, meaning anyone can view the computer code and create their own version of the application.

Applications like BitTorrent do not have to be open source and the developers of the application are the only people that can view the source code.

dApps run on a blockchain

On the Ethereum network, dApps run on a blockchain, which allows functionality that is not possible for standard applications.

Blockchain technology is covered earlier in this book.

dApps have an in-app currency or token

The Ethereum platform requires developers to pay for computing power with the Ether currency in order to make apps profitable and cover the costs of computing power. dApps running on Ethereum can create their own in-app tokens, which users can purchase and exchange for functions in the application.

For example, sending a message in a messaging app may require 1 token. This token may only be a fraction of a cent, so it does not cost a significant amount to send a message. However, it's not free like current messaging apps.

Decentralized changes to the app

While there are developers that create the dApps, once they have released it, changes to the app and decisions about the app are decided by the majority of users.

This is a danger of dApps and decentralized networks: the control of the app or network is in the hands of the majority of the network.

Anyone can edit the code of an open-source application and release their own version. If the majority of users select to run that version of the application, then it becomes the main version of the app.

Final Chapter Notes on dApps

You should now have an understanding about what dApps are and how they work. In the next chapter, we'll look at smart contracts on Ethereum.

Chapter 6: Smart Contracts

Smart Contracts

Smart contracts that operate on a blockchain are another major innovation introduced by Ethereum. Blockchain-based smart contracts have been hailed as a revolutionary concept that could impact global finance, contracts, and almost every industry in the world.

What are smart contracts?

Smart contracts are enforceable contracts that are much like legal contract; however, instead of being written by lawyers and enforced by courts, they are written in computer code and can be self-enforcing.

Traditional contracts

Traditional contracts are generally written by lawyers and contain pages of terms and conditions of an agreement between two parties. They contain the details about what was agreed upon along with compensation and consequences for breaking the terms of the contract.

If one of the parties in the contact doesn't fulfil their side of the contract, the other party may hire a lawyer and take them to court to claim compensation.

The terms of the contract may be ambiguous, with grammar playing an impact on the interpretation of a contract. There have been cases where a single comma has changed the meaning of a sentence in a contract.

A recent example of this was the case of Oxhurst Dairy, where the company was taken to court for $10 million dollars of unpaid overtime due to a disagreement over a sentence where a missing comma changed the meaning of the sentence.

Court cases are lengthy and expensive and even if the court case is won, there is no guarantee compensation will be received. At the very least, the entire process will take a lot of time and money before it is resolved.

How smart contracts work:

Smart contracts are written in computer code using the Solidity programming language; there is no ambiguity in the terms of a computer code. Smart contracts run on the Ethereum Virtual Machine and Ethereum blockchain, connected to the Ethereum cryptocurrency Ether.

The terms of a contract can contain payment amounts along with compensation for failure to complete the terms of the contract, all written in computer code.

If there is a contract for the sale of a company, the smart contract would contain ownership of the shares of the company and ownership rights. Payment would be sent to the smart contract, not directly to the seller. Once the smart contract receives the payment, it would transfer ownership of the company to the buyer and the funds for the purchase to the seller.

If the buyer doesn't pay the full amount or payment is not received before the expiry date, the smart contract would transfer the shares and ownership back to the seller, cancel the contract and reject any future payments sent to it.

Benefits of smart contracts:

- Existing legal contracts can be ambiguous depending on the words and grammar used. Smart contracts are written in computer code so there should be less misunderstanding about the wording and terms in a smart contract.

- There are no lawyers or courts required to enforce the contract. If the terms of a contract are met, the contract is executed. If the terms of the contract are not met, then the terms of breaking the contract are automatically executed and compensation is paid.

- Smart contracts run on the decentralized Ethereum network. As mentioned earlier, this reduces the risk of hacking, fraud, server downtime and unauthorised access to the contracts.

- The level of autonomy of the contract can be determined. Smart contracts can be a combination of partially or fully self-executing and self-enforcing.

- Edits and changes to a smart contract are all recorded on the blockchain. This creates an immutable record of all changes and actions that have occurred to the smart contract.

- Smart contracts have a wide range of uses. A large number of companies are developing smart contracts that could improve the way existing industries and processes run.

Disadvantages/dangers of smart contracts:

- Lawyers are replaced with computer programmers. While anyone can create a smart contract, very few people will have the skills required to write one themselves. Computer programmers will be required to create them instead of lawyers.

- Errors in computer code could be worse than ambiguous words in a contract. If there are ambiguous words in a contract, it can be discussed, amended, debated or taken to court. If there is an error in the computer code in a contract, the contract will run the code with the error and it can't be reversed or taken to court. This was the case of the DAO, where bad wording in the smart contract caused the loss of $50 million.

- You can't argue with a smart contract. The contract will enforce the terms based on the code. There is no judge to determine whether the terms are fair or appeals court to challenge any decision. If a party feels the contract was unfair or was executed incorrectly due to error or a misunderstanding of the terms, there are no avenues to challenge the contract. This also occurred with the DAO, where a hard fork and new version of Ethereum was required to reverse the smart contract.

- There is a limit to the types of contracts that can be created. Digital ownership of assets can be determined; however, it may be more difficult for real-world assets. It may also be difficult for smart contracts to determine whether the quality of work was up to the standard expected. Basic yes-and-no requirements could be programmed, such as, “Was one hour of work completed?” However, the quality of that work may not be able to be determined.

- Software problems could cause errors in the smart contract. Smart contracts run on Ethereum, which relies on a network of computers and software to operate. Problems with the software or network could cause errors in smart contracts.

- Jurisdiction for enforcement of the smart contract can be unclear. Smart contracts are computer code that can exist without legal jurisdiction of a country or state. If there is a breach of contract or dispute about the terms of the contract, the smart contract may have no legal jurisdiction other than the blockchain. It is possible that any arbitration that may be possible would occur in a blockchain arbitration court handled by computer code, as proposed by the company CodeLegit.

- It is an untested method for creating and enforcing contracts. Legal contracts have been used for hundreds of years; they may not be perfect but they’ve stood the test of time. Smart contracts are new and haven’t been proven over a long period of time. Using smart contracts at this early stage may expose businesses to unexpected risks associated with a new technology.

End of chapter notes on smart contracts

Smart contracts offer many advantages over existing contracts; however, there are also significant downsides associated with them. Smart contracts are still a new concept so the implications and problems with using smart contracts are still being discovered.

Chapter 7: Benefits of Ethereum

Giant World Supercomputer

One of the most impressive advantages of Ethereum is that all the individual computers connected together act like one giant worldwide supercomputer.

While the Bitcoin network is also connected like a worldwide supercomputer, the computing power of the Bitcoin network is directed towards processing transactions.

The computing power on the Ethereum network can be directed towards the Ethereum Virtual Machine. This allows applications to run, utilizing the power of one of the most powerful supercomputers in the world.

Ethereum Virtual Machine

Blockchain technology is revolutionary; however, prior to Ethereum, blockchains had limited capabilities and were mainly used for recording transactions.

One of the important innovations that Ethereum offered over existing blockchain technology was the Ethereum Virtual Machine (EVM).

The Ethereum Virtual Machine allowed developers to create applications in computer programming languages similar to languages they are familiar with. These applications can be as advanced as any applications they could create on other computer platforms. They are run on the Ethereum Virtual Machine, which allows these decentralized applications to use blockchain technology with greater ease and lower costs than previously possible.

Ease of development

Creating a blockchain network is expensive, time consuming, and complicated, as it requires many people to contribute computing power to a new blockchain network.

Developers must create a new blockchain and build a network of computers and users that would support it.

Ethereum allows developers to utilize the existing Ethereum blockchain and network of computers. The Ethereum Virtual Machine also allows developers to create applications on blockchain technology, without needing to create their own blockchain network.

Developing applications that run on the Ethereum blockchain and EVM is relatively easy. The programming language is similar to commonly used programming languages, such as JavaScript. As the programming language is similar to existing programming languages, developers can create programs easily with minimal additional learning.

Decentralization

We may think we control our Facebook photos, computer files in cloud storage, or the messages in our chat application. However, these are controlled by centralized systems and companies.

When you upload photos to Facebook, all your images are stored on a central server owned by Facebook. This is the same for files you upload to Google drive or other cloud storage.

When you send a message using a chat application, the message is sent to the central servers of the company, which then sends it from the server to the message recipient. The servers keep a record of all the messages. When you access your chat history, you access it from those servers.

Ethereum allows for the decentralization of applications and data, meaning there is no central server or company that controls all your data. Decentralized applications are run across a network of computers; if one computer goes offline, the data can be accessed from the other computers also running the application.

Many applications and websites we are familiar with today are being developed as decentralized versions on the Ethereum network. This includes decentralized cloud storage, messaging applications, social networks and more.

No Censorship

The decentralized structure of the Ethereum network means governments and companies can't censor websites and applications.

If a government wanted to censor a website, they could block access to the website or close the server running the website. If they wanted to censor a decentralized application, they would have to shut down every computer or server running that application.

The computers running dApps are spread across the entire world, making it impossible for one government to shut them all down.

If a user posts an image on twitter, Facebook, or Instagram that the company doesn't approve of, they can remove the image and ban the user. This may not seem like a problem for most people, as they aren't posting anything against the rules of these companies. However, these companies must obey the laws within the countries they operate. Most social media platforms are banned in China, as foreign companies don't comply with the harsh censorship of the Chinese governments.

Users that post content that mentions Tibet, the Tiananmen Square massacre, or anything critical of the Chinese government will have that content removed in China. They may also be investigated by the Chinese government after posting it. Companies operating in China must ban content the government doesn't approve of and provide user data to the government.

With a decentralized network and applications, companies and governments can't censor content, ban applications, or obtain user data. This provides greater freedom of speech and puts control back in the hands of the users of applications running on Ethereum.

Security

Many risks involved with existing centralized systems are greatly reduced with decentralized systems.

Facebook, PayPal, banks, and most other companies have centralized servers. If those servers are hacked, then hackers may obtain all your personal data stored on those servers. If the central servers crash or go offline, then all the data is inaccessible.

Decentralized servers are not as vulnerable to hacking or server failure. To hack a decentralized system, the hacker would need to control the majority of the computing power on the network. As the Ethereum network is hundreds of thousands of computers all over the world, it is almost impossible for someone to control the majority of the network.

Smart Contracts

Smart contracts are contracts written in computer code, they can execute automatically if the terms of a contract are met. There are no lawyers or courts required to enforce the terms of a contract.

While Bitcoin allowed payments across a blockchain, these payments were manual, such as selecting to send money to another person. Ethereum has allowed automatic payments that can be triggered when an event, milestone, or condition occurs.

When you take a taxi, at the end of the trip, you may pay the driver with cash. Bitcoin could replace cash as a payment method by allowing you to pay with Bitcoin, instead of cash. Bitcoin is limited to manual payments and transactions, like this example.

If we use the example of Uber, your credit card details are stored with Uber. When you start a trip, you contract to pay an amount based on the distance travelled. When you finish your trip, the contract executes, and your credit card is automatically charged for the trip.

Ethereum has created a platform where decentralized apps (dApps) could run with smart contracts to replace this process. Instead of the Uber app, you could use a dApp that automatically executes smart contracts based on the distance travelled. This would work similar to the Uber example above, but it would operate on the Ethereum platform using Ether or an Ethereum token as payment.

This is one potential application of dApps and smart contracts. There are thousands of dApps in development that could change a wide range of industries.

New methods for funding companies and projects

Ethereum has opened new possibilities for companies and developers to raise money to fund their growth. While Initial Coin Offerings were possible before Ethereum, these were linked to the popularity of a new cryptocurrency.

Ethereum allows companies to develop applications and sell tokens or coins that can be used in the applications. These applications run on the Ethereum platform, and if an app becomes popular, the tokens used in the application should theoretically increase in value.

Companies can raise funds for their projects, without requiring loans or venture capital funding. Initial supporters of an application can also profit if the app becomes popular.

End of Chapter Notes on the Benefits of Ethereum

There are other benefits that Ethereum offers; however, many of these are also related to the underlying blockchain technology, which is not unique to Ethereum. While Ethereum provides many benefits, there are also many downsides. In the next chapter, we'll cover some disadvantages and risks of Ethereum.

Chapter 8: Disadvantages and Risks of Ethereum

While the benefits and potential of Ethereum is impressive, there are also many disadvantages and risks associated with it. In this chapter, we'll cover some dangers and risks of Ethereum.

Ether is not designed for real world transactions

Ether, the cryptocurrency used for payments on the Ethereum network, is used to pay for computing power to run dApps and smart contracts. Ether is not designed to be used for payments at shops, online, or as an alternative to other real-world payment methods.

Bitcoin and many other cryptocurrencies are more practical forms of payment with many accepted at shops and websites around the world. Using Ether will depend on the popularity of the Ethereum platform and the number of people running dApps and smart contracts.

Ether May Not Increase in Value

Even if the Ethereum platform gains in popularity, there is no guarantee the price of Ether will increase. Many people buying Ether are purchasing it for speculative profit and do not intend to use it for running dApps or smart contracts.

The current price of Ether may be overvalued by traders and speculators. If they sell, this may dramatically decrease the price of Ether.

Even if developers and companies use the Ethereum platform, the price of Ether may not increase if there is a greater supply of Ether created or demand from traders decreases.

New and Unproven Technology

Ethereum is a new technology. While it has a lot of potential, there are still many unknown risks involved with any new technology.

While many companies have joined an alliance to develop the use of Ethereum within their organizations, this is still at the research and feasibility stage. There have been few companies implementing Ethereum as a replacement for existing systems. There have also been a few mainstream dApps that have become popular.

Many dangers and risks involved with using Ethereum may still be unknown and may not become apparent until Ethereum is being used on a larger scale.

Issues with Smart Contracts

Smart contracts have a lot of benefits; however, there are also significant dangers with using smart contracts.

The biggest case that highlights the flaws in smart contracts is the DAO hack, as mentioned earlier. A badly written smart contract allowed a group of people to exploit the contract and steal more than 50 million dollars.

Thousands of people looked at the code in the DAO smart contract, and most saw no issues. The problems with the smart contract were only realized after they had been exploited.

With a standard legal contract, if there is poorly written wording that allows someone to exploit the contract, this can be taken to court. The disagreement over the wording and intention of a contract can be settled through legal proceedings.

This is not the case with smart contracts. Once a smart contract executes, it can't be argued with or reversed. There are no lawyers or courts to challenge a smart contract.

Dangers of a Giant Worldwide Supercomputer

If you've seen the Terminator movies, you know that Skynet is a worldwide computer network. When Skynet was activated, it detected humanity as a threat and waged war against humans.

The Ethereum network and smart contracts have been compared to Skynet. Ethereum is a worldwide network of computers that are connected, running applications and code that can't be argued with.

In the DAO hack, people exploited a vulnerability in the code of a smart contract to steal more than 50 million dollars. While there are financial risks with smart contracts, there are also much greater security risks.

Smart contracts are being designed for almost everything, including connecting to household appliances, cars, phones, and other electronic systems.

Computer systems are used by almost every modern army today, with some of the most advanced weapons relying heavily on computer technology. Governments are now looking to implement blockchain based technology to replace their existing database systems.

If there was an error in code or the code was badly written, it opens the possibility that the smart contract doesn't run as intended. The contract could then run without being stopped or altered, leading to potentially disastrous consequences, especially if connected to government or military systems.

Hype around dApps

dApps offer many benefits over existing applications. However, throughout history, there have been many technologies with benefits over existing options but failed to gain mainstream adoption.

Applications, such as Instagram and Facebook, are free; however, they use your personal information to allow advertisers to sell products and services to you. They are free for you to use, but your personal data is the product these companies are selling to other people.

dApps are controlled by the users, not by a centralized company. The users control their privacy and data. In exchange for this control, using the dApp will generally cost money. Uploading a photo, liking a photo, and other actions on a photo sharing dApp may cost a certain amount of money for each action.

Convincing people to pay for a new application that is similar to a more popular free application they use may be difficult. Privacy and the benefits of decentralization may not be compelling enough reasons for people to use dApps over existing applications, especially if it will cost them money to use them.

End of Chapter Notes on the Disadvantages and Risks of Ethereum

These are just some dangers and risks of the Ethereum platform. Ethereum is still new, and many dangers and risks may still be unknown. dApps and smart contracts have a long way to go before they gain mainstream acceptance. It is still possible that they never actually gain mainstream acceptance.

The future of Ethereum is still uncertain, and in the next chapter, we’ll look at some factors that could determine the future of Ethereum.

Chapter 9: Setting up an Ethereum wallet

The first requirement before you can use the Ethereum network is to set up an Ethereum wallet. There are a variety of wallets you can set up, each with different advantages and disadvantages.

In this chapter, we'll cover the different types of wallets and how to get started with Ethereum.

Important Notes and Warnings

When setting up a wallet, it's crucial you pay attention to the set-up process and record any passwords, phrases, private keys, and information.

Setting up a cryptocurrency wallet is different from setting up a bank account or online account. If you lose your passwords or recovery phrases, there is no way to recover them. For most wallet types, there is also no company you can contact to reset any passwords you forget.

Forgetting passwords or not backing up recovery phrases is one of the biggest reasons people lose their cryptocurrencies.

It's also important to store your passwords and backup phrases on a different device than your wallet. If you lose your computer or phone and the only backup of your recovery phrases is on the same device, then you will also lose access to your wallet.

This point can't be stressed enough, so please make sure, if there are passwords or recovery phrases when setting up a wallet, you back them up and store them in a safe location separate to the device your wallet is on.

What is an Ethereum wallet?

An Ethereum wallet consists of a few main components:

- Ethereum address: This is similar to an email address. You provide your Ethereum address to other people, so they can send you Ether, just like you would provide your email address to other people, so they can email you.

  Your Ethereum address is public. Everyone on the Ethereum network can view your balance and all transactions that have occurred on your address.

An Ethereum wallet can hold multiple addresses.

- Private Key: A private key is the password used to prove ownership of your Ethereum address to access it and transfer Ether from the address.

  Important Note: Do not provide your private key to anyone. This is the equivalent of providing the pin code to your bank card. Anyone with your private key has authority over your address and can transfer Ether out of your address.

- Client / Software: To access your wallet and make transactions, you will need software or a way to access your wallet and communicate with the Ethereum network. This is known as client, which may be a mobile app, website, or computer software that connects to the network.

  This is similar to how you would access your bank account and make transactions using the mobile app or website for your bank.

Ethereum tokens and ICOs

ICOs and Ethereum tokens are covered in more detail later in the book; however, we'll briefly mention them here, as they are an important factor when deciding which wallet to use.

ICO stands for "Initial Coin Offering." It is when a new coin is offered to the public previously not available for purchase or exchange. Commonly, these new coins are tokens that use the Ethereum platform.

Ethereum Tokens

Ethereum tokens are similar to cryptocurrencies; however, they do not have their own blockchain or computer network like cryptocurrencies. They utilize the existing Ethereum blockchain and network and operate on top of it.

Generally, Ethereum tokens are used within a decentralized app running on Ethereum.

Ethereum tokens are covered in greater detail later in the book; however, for now, it is important to note that only certain types of wallets allow you to hold Ethereum tokens and participate in ICOs. Wallets that allow you to hold Ethereum tokens will be outlined in this chapter.

Quick Getting Started Method

If you haven't used Ethereum and are looking for the easiest way to get started and buy Ethereum, a quick method is below:

- Open a hybrid web wallet combined with an exchange like Coinbase.
- You can buy Ether after setting up your Coinbase account using existing payment methods. This is a quick and easy way to buy your first Ether.
- Coinbase doesn't allow you to participate in ICOs or hold Ethereum tokens, so after setting up a Coinbase account and purchasing Ether, you may want to set up another wallet if you wish to hold tokens.
- You can set up a mobile app or software wallet that provides different features and benefits, such as MyEtherWallet, Jaxx, or Exodus.
- You can then transfer Ether from Coinbase to your new wallet.

Wallet Types

There are a range of wallet types for holding and transacting on the Ethereum network. Each type of wallet has different benefits and disadvantages, which we'll cover in this section.

This list covers the main wallet types and a few options for each type. The options are the most popular or easy to use for each category; however, there are more apps, software, and websites than the ones listed below.

Web Wallet

A web wallet is a wallet that can be accessed from a web browser on a computer or mobile. It is similar to logging into internet banking in a web browser on your computer.

Web wallets can be used by beginners or experienced cryptocurrency users.

They can be set up in minutes from a web browser with no ID verification required.

Web wallets require no applications or software to be installed. Any updates to the web wallet are done by the website on their servers, so you need not update or download new versions of the web wallet.

Web wallets provide you access to your private keys. There is generally no customer service or company to contact if you lose your private keys. Make sure you backup your private keys and take care of them; otherwise, you will lose access to your web wallet.

Web wallets are like any other website. They can be blocked by governments or internet providers. Scam sites can create copies of legitimate web wallets and have similar names to trick people into logging into the wrong site and revealing their private keys. Websites can also be hacked, so while the site might be legitimate, there may be malicious code inserted in the website that can steal private keys.

You may not purchase Ethereum directly through a web wallet, so you may need to set up another wallet to purchase Ethereum. There are services to purchase Ethereum and transfer it to your web wallet; however, they may also require verification of ID. Some web wallets allow you to hold Ethereum tokens and participate in ICOs.

Popular Ethereum web wallets:

My Ether Wallet: www.myetherwallet.com

My Ether Wallet is the most popular and trustworthy Ethereum wallet, it also allows you to hold Ethereum tokens and participate in ICOs.

Note: There are scam sites attempting to copy My Ether Wallet, so double check the website address and security certificate to ensure you are on the correct site.

Exchange

Exchanges are similar to stock market exchanges or currency trading exchanges. They allow traders to buy and sell cryptocurrencies from each other to profit from price changes.

With an exchange, you can hold many cryptocurrencies in the same account and trade between them easily. They are generally regulated, like financial institutions. They may also have features, such as customer support and security methods, similar to traditional online banking websites.

You don't control your private keys with an exchange. While this reduces the chance of you losing your private keys, it opens you up to other risks, such as the exchange being hacked or going bankrupt. This occurred with the largest Bitcoin exchange Mt.Gox. While it is less of a risk now, as exchanges are more regulated, the risk still exists.

Exchanges allow you to buy cryptocurrencies using traditional payment methods; however, they have extensive verification procedures. You can use exchanges without going through long verification processes by funding your account with cryptocurrencies you already have.

Popular Ethereum Exchanges:
Poloniex: www.poloniex.com
Kraken www.kraken.com
GDAX: www.gdax.com
Bittrex: www.bittrex.com

Hybrid Web Wallet / Exchange

A hybrid web wallet / exchange combines the features of a Ethereum web wallet with an exchange. It provides the ability to send and receive Ether like a web wallet, along with buying or sell Ether at exchange market prices.

Hybrid web wallets / exchanges allow you to purchase Ether using traditional payment methods, such as bank accounts and credit cards. They are generally regulated similar to other financial institutions and require verification of identity before you can make purchases.

As a hybrid web wallet is a combination of web wallet and exchange, it does not offer the full features of either. The web wallet functionality is not as complete as other web wallets, and the exchange functionality is not as feature rich as other exchanges.

You cannot hold Ethereum tokens or participate in ICOs using a hybrid web wallet / exchange. You also don't control your private keys, so it's important to use a regulated, trustworthy company.

When getting started with Ethereum, a hybrid web wallet / exchange is often the best option. It provides a user-friendly interface that doesn't require an understanding of complicated wallet features or exchange trading. It also provides an easy way to buy Ether quickly, using existing payment methods.

Popular Ethereum Web Wallets/ Exchanges:
Coinbase: http://bit.ly/10freebitcoin ($10 free bitcoin when using this link)

Coinbase is one of the largest and most reliable web wallets / exchanges. It is highly regulated, like other financial institutions, and makes purchasing Ether quick and easy for beginners.

As it is regulated, like standard financial institutions, it requires ID verification before you make purchases.

Mobile Apps
Everyone that has a smartphone has used a mobile app. There are apps for everything these days, including Ethereum wallet apps. These apps may allow you to buy, sell, send, and receive Ethereum, with other cryptocurrencies from your smartphone.

Mobile apps are easy to install and use, like any other mobile app. They provide the convenience of having access to your cryptocurrency wallet in your smartphone and are generally more secure than other options, as they must pass security requirements set by the app stores.

As apps must pass certain app store requirements, they rarely allow you to hold Ethereum tokens or purchase Ether from within the app.

When setting up your mobile app, it's important to store your backup data, private keys, and recovery phrases on another device, not on your phone. A common mistake is storing all backup and recovery data on the same device as the wallet. If this device is lost, stolen, or broken then the wallet and your recovery data is lost.

Popular Ethereum Mobile Wallets:
Coinbase – Does not allow Ethereum tokens
Jaxx – Does not allow all Ethereum tokens

Software
While mobile apps and web apps are becoming increasingly more popular than computer software, most people still use computer software daily.

Software wallets allow you to install and manage an Ethereum wallet from your computer or laptop. They are a little more difficult to install and set up; however, if you've ever installed computer software, you should have no problem installing them.

Software installed from the internet may pose higher security risks than a mobile app, so be careful to check where you are downloading the software from.

Software wallets can run on computer and laptop monitors, so they have a larger, easier to use design compared to mobile. They may also allow you to hold multiple cryptocurrencies and tokens within your wallet.

It's important to put a password on your computer and your software wallet. It's also essential to store your private keys and recovery phrases on a different device or cloud storage, so they are not on your computer.

A big risk of software wallets is not correctly storing passwords and recovery phrases on a different device. If your computer is stolen, broken, or gets a virus and your only recovery phrases are on the same computer as your wallet, then you will lose access to your wallet.

Popular Ethereum Software wallets:
Exodus: https://www.exodus.io/
Jaxx: https://jaxx.io/

Chrome Extensions

Chrome extensions are applications that run within the Google Chrome web browser. They can do almost anything a website or software can do and are accessible from the menu bar of a web browser.

There are Ethereum wallet chrome extensions that allow you to send and receive Ether from within your web browser. An advantage of chrome extensions is they can provide enhanced functionality to websites you visit by detecting Ether addresses on pages or connecting to web apps.

There are significant security risks with chrome extensions, as they are easy to create and release on the chrome store. While they can provide enhanced functionality to web pages, they may also read the data you enter on websites. Installing chrome extensions with security flaws or malicious extensions could put your personal and financial data at risk, so be careful to install only trusted extensions.

While chrome extensions have the convenience of being in your web browser, you can only access them from that web browser. They are not like web wallets, where you can access them from any device with an internet connection.

This means, if you lose your computer, it breaks, or is stolen, you will lose access to your wallet if you have no backup of your passwords and recovery phrases on another device.

Popular Ethereum Chrome Extensions:
MetaMask: https://metamask.io/

Jaxx: https://jaxx.io/

Paper Wallet

A paper wallet is a wallet printed on a piece of paper. The piece of paper will contain the public address and QR code for the wallet, which can be provided to other people to send money to that wallet. When a paper wallet is printed, it may also have the private key on it. Make sure you remove the private key and keep the private key separate.

Paper wallets are not connected to a computer, website, or electronic network so they are not vulnerable to many risks of software or web-based wallets. Paper wallets can't be hacked and provide a cold storage option for securely storing Ether.

As they are not connected to the Ethereum network, you can't send transactions unless you enter your private keys in a website or software, which can then open it up to security risks.

Paper wallets are easy to lose, steal, or destroy so they should be laminated to reduce these risks. Private keys should be stored securely in multiple locations, separate from the public wallet information.

Popular Ethereum web wallets:
My Ether Wallet: www.myetherwallet.com

My Ether Wallet allows you to generate a paper wallet. You can only send transactions if you import the private key into a website or software.

Note: There are scam sites attempting to copy My Ether Wallet, so double check the website address and security certificate to ensure you are on the correct site.

Hardware wallet
Hardware wallets are electronic devices that store the private keys for an Ethereum or cryptocurrency wallet. They have similar security features to a paper wallet as they are not connected to the network unless sending a transaction, so Ether is held in cold storage most of the time.

Hardware wallets must be connected to a computer to send transactions, which may expose them to some security risks. Hardware wallets are generally designed so the private key is not exposed when sending transactions. Some hardware wallets may allow you to hide wallets with large balances, in case of theft or a situation where you are forced to expose the balance of your hardware wallet.

You can't purchase Ether using a hardware wallet, and they may not allow you to hold tokens. You must have another way of obtaining Ether first and then transfer it to your hardware wallet.

Hardware wallets are generally recommended for people experienced with Ethereum and cryptocurrencies.

Popular Ethereum Hardware Wallets:
Trezor: www.trezor.io
Ledger: www.ledgerwallet.com
KeepKey: www.keepkey.com

End of Chapter Notes on Ethereum Wallets

Ethereum wallets may be confusing at first; hopefully, this chapter has helped you understand the different wallets available and provided you some options for setting them up.

When setting up an Ethereum wallet, remember it's important to keep secure backups of your private key and recovery phrase. If you lose your private key or recovery phrase, then you will lose access to your wallet and the funds in it.

Later in the book, we'll cover how to buy, send, and use Ether, along with how to correctly participate in an ICO.

Chapter 10: Buying, Sending, Receiving, and Trading Ether

After setting up an Ethereum wallet, you'll be ready to use the Ethereum network. In this chapter, we'll cover how to buy, send, receive, exchange, and use Ether.

Buying Ether

Buying Ether using traditional payment methods, such as credit card or bank transfer, may be the easiest way to get started owning Ether.

There are several ways you can buy Ether. If you set up a Coinbase account, you can easily buy Ether through Coinbase. The process is simple, and the Ether will be instantly credited to your wallet after purchasing it.

If you set up an account with an exchange, such as Kraken, you can also buy Ether using traditional a credit card or bank transfer. Your Kraken account has a wallet to hold your Ether, so after purchase, it will be in your account immediately.

If you haven't set up a wallet with Coinbase or Kraken, another open to buy Ether using a credit card is Changelly. This website allows you to exchange different cryptocurrencies and to purchase cryptocurrencies using a credit card.

You can purchase Ether using a credit card with Changelly at www.changelly.com

To receive the Ether with Changelly, you must have an existing wallet to receive Ether, which we'll cover in the next section.

Receiving Ether

To receive Ether into your wallet, you must provide your address to the person or service sending Ether to you. This is like providing your bank account details to someone, so they can transfer money into that account.

There are two main ways you can supply this address, either by the providing the public key (public address), which is a unique group of letters and numbers, or by providing the QR code.

Your Ethereum address will look similar to the below letters and numbers:

0x3035eE16a1CB8484Af86356D7d9C0cdbf1582957

With a service like Changelly, you must enter your Ethereum address to receive Ether. After purchasing the Ether, it will be sent to your address.

Note: Do not confuse your private key with your public address. They look very similar. Make sure you are providing your correct public address when giving it to someone else and never give your private key to anyone.

Providing your address is fine if it can be copied and pasted. As you can see from the address shown earlier, if this address was typed, it could be easy to make a mistake and send Ether to the wrong address. If the address can't be copied and pasted, then providing your QR code might be a better option to ensure it is sent to the correct address.

A QR code is a Quick Response code that acts like a barcode, containing information that can quickly be scanned and read by different applications. You may have seen the square boxes that look like a square barcode before directing you to a website by scanning the square box with an app on your smartphone camera.

Sending Ether

Sending Ether is similar to receiving Ether. You will require either the Ethereum address or the QR code to send Ether.

In your Ether wallet, you can select "Send" usually by pressing a send button. You will then be prompted to enter the amount of Ether to send and the address to send it to.

The amount of Ether may be a dollar amount, but more commonly, it is a unit amount such as 1 Ether or 0.5 Ether etc.

You can copy and paste the address to send the Ether to or scan the QR code. It's important to double check the address is correct, because if you send

Ether to the wrong address, there is no way to reverse the transaction, and you could lose your Ether.

After checking the amount to send and the address are correct, you can send the Ether to the recipient.

Trading / Exchanging Ether

After buying or receiving Ether, you may want to trade or exchange your Ether for other cryptocurrencies.

You can trade Ether using an exchange, such as Kraken or Poloniex, as you would trade stocks or currencies. You can use your Ether to buy other cryptocurrencies, which will be held in a wallet for each cryptocurrency on the exchange.

This can be an easy way to obtain and hold a range of different cryptocurrencies in one account. Trading cryptocurrencies to profit from price fluctuations is highly speculative and involves a large amount of risk.

Ether can be exchanged for other cryptocurrencies using Changelly (www.changelly.com) or Shapeshift (www.shapeshift.io).

Exchanging Ether for other cryptocurrencies using these services involves sending Ether to an address, selecting the cryptocurrency to receive in exchange, and the address to send that cryptocurrency to.

Software and mobile app wallets, such as Jaxx and Exodus, include Shapeshift exchange functionality built into their wallets. This allows you to exchange Ether for other cryptocurrencies from directly within the wallet.

Exchanging Ether for computing power

Ether can be exchanged for computing power to run decentralized applications and smart contracts on the Ethereum network. Using Ether for running dApps and smart contracts is a more advanced topic that won't be covered in this book. However, it's worth noting Ether has this practical use for many developers and companies.

End of Chapter Notes on Buying, Sending, Receiving, and Trading Ether

You should now understand how to set up a wallet along with how to buy, send, and receive Ether.

Initial Coin Offerings (ICOs) have become popular recently, with many people exchanging Ether to apply for new cryptocurrency coins and tokens. Later in the book, we'll cover the wallet required and how to apply for ICOs.

Chapter 11: ICOs and Ethereum Tokens

ICOs have become a popular way for companies and developers to raise money to fund development of applications or businesses. In this chapter, we'll cover what ICOs are, how they work, and their dangers.

What is an ICO?

ICO is an acronym for "Initial Coin Offering." It is when developers or a company raise money by offering a new coin or token for purchase. This may be a new cryptocurrency or a token on the Ethereum platform that can be used in an application.

We'll cover how ICOs work later in this chapter, but first, we'll cover Ethereum tokens to understand what is being offered in an ICO.

Ethereum Tokens

Ethereum tokens are used in an dApp built on the Ethereum platform. You may be familiar with iPhone and Android apps and games that allow you to access levels or purchase upgrades and bonuses within the application. Real money is exchanged for gold or tokens in an application that allows you to buy items in the app. This is similar to how tokens work on the Ethereum platform.

Developers create decentralized applications that run on Ethereum. The currency Ether is exchanged for tokens that can be used in these applications. For example, in a decentralized messaging app, Ether can be exchanged for the tokens of the messaging app. These tokens can then be used in the messaging app to send messages and access other features.

Unlike mobile games and apps, where there is an unlimited number of credits that can be purchased, the number of tokens available for an Ethereum dApp is limited. As the number of tokens is limited, the price will change based on the usage and popularity of that application. The more people use the app, the more tokens they must purchase from the existing supply of tokens. The supply of tokens is limited, so as demand increases, the price of the tokens will increase in value. Users that purchased tokens early will have more abilities in the application and will profit from the increase in value if they resell the tokens to other users.

How ICOs work

ICOs work by offering coins or tokens to people before an app is launched. People exchange Ether or Bitcoin for tokens that can be used in the application. The developers or company raise money to fund the development of the app.

The idea behind an ICO is that, if a company develops an app that becomes popular, the tokens will increase in value, and the people that purchased the tokens in the ICO will profit.

The developers can raise money for the app to pay wages, without selling shares in a company or borrowing money.

Dangers / Risks of ICOs

There are significant risks of participating in an ICO, which we'll cover in this section.

Loss of initial investment

Perhaps the biggest risk is the loss of the money you invest in the ICO. This could be due to several reasons. While you may be aware losing your investment is a risk, it is the reasons you may lose your money you may be unaware of.

Developers never create an app

Many ICOs raise money to fund the development of an application. There is no guarantee they will actually build an app. Creating software is time consuming and costly, and the developers may run out of money before they can create anything.

The app is not popular

Even if the developers can create an app, there is no guarantee the app will be popular or that anyone will want to use the app.

If very few people are using the app, then the tokens won't go up in value and may even fall in value. Over time, the tokens may become worthless, as nobody wants to use the app; therefore, nobody needs to buy the tokens.

The tokens don't go up in value

If the developers create an app and people use it, there is still the risk the tokens don't go up in value.

There may have been a lot of tokens sold in the ICO, which creates an excessive supply of tokens. While people may use the app, the demand for tokens may not be enough to increase the price of the tokens.

No secondary market

It is easy for a company to create a token and offer it to the public. Once you buy those tokens in an ICO, there is no guarantee you can sell them again to get your money back.

If you can't sell your tokens, then you can't get your money back or profit from them. You may only use them in an app, which is only possible if the developers create an app in the first place.

Legal and regulatory risks

China has recently banned ICOs and moved to close cryptocurrency exchanges. Part of the ban on ICOs that China implemented was for any companies that raised funds via an ICO to return funds to the people that purchased tokens.

There are guidelines and rules in most countries about creating companies and offering shares to investors, and ICOs attempt to get around these regulations.

While ICOs have been allowed so far, this is mainly due to the fact they are a new technology where regulation doesn't yet exist. The Securities and Exchange Commission (SEC) in the U.S with financial regulatory institutions in other countries are examining ICOs with companies that raise funds via ICOs and will likely implement regulation.

While companies may raise funds now in an ICO, they may face legal and regulatory issues in the future. These regulations may be applied retrospectively, as in China, which may affect any companies that raised funds through an ICO in the past. This could cause companies to lose money and tokens for their apps to become worthless.

Scams

While there are many legitimate companies raising money in ICOs, there are also a large number of outright scams.

There are no regulations for companies raising funds using ICOs. This has allowed scammers to create websites and steal money from people unaware of the difference between a legitimate ICO and a scam.

Scammers have created websites and social media accounts that copy legitimate ICOs. This has created confusion on which is the real company, leading many people to send money to the wrong company.

Even ICOs that seem unique and legitimate may be set up by people with no intention of using money raised to build applications. They may just raise the money for themselves and claim the project or company failed. As there is no regulation, there is nothing stopping people from doing this and no legal ramifications.

Incorrect address or wallet

Another risk of applying for ICOs is sending and receiving funds. If you send funds to or from the wrong address, you may lose your funds.

If the wallet or address you put to receive the tokens isn't the correct type, you may also lose your funds.

Most ICOs require a special type of Ethereum wallet that allows you to hold tokens within the wallet. Often, the address you send funds from is the address tokens will be sent to. If this is an address that can't hold tokens, when the tokens are sent, they will be lost.

Participating in an ICO

If after reading all those risks, you still want to participate in an ICO, you must be careful to do it correctly. In this section, we'll cover the wallet required and understand the basics of applying for an ICO.

Wallet required to apply for an ICO

You need a special wallet that allows you to hold tokens when applying for an ICO.

Exchanges, such as Poloniex and kraken, with hybrid web wallets, such as Coinbase, don't allow you to receive tokens from an ICO. Do not send Bitcoin or Ethereum from these platforms, as you will lose your funds and not receive your tokens.

To apply for an ICO, you will need a wallet from a site or software such as:

My Ether Wallet - myetherwallet.com

Meta Mask - metamask.io

These wallets allow you to send Ether and receive and hold tokens. There are other wallets that allow you to send Ether and receive tokens; however, the above are generally the most common wallets recommended on ICO websites.

Don't send funds before the ICO opens

ICOs will generally have a countdown time before the ICO starts. They will usually not release the address to send funds to before the ICO opens.

Sometimes, the address will be released a few hours before to give people time to prepare; however, any applications sent before the official opening time will not be accepted, and funds may be lost.

Sending Ether to an ICO

If you hold Ether in MyEtherWallet or MetaMask wallets mentioned earlier, you may receive the tokens onto the same address.

Generally, the process is that, once the ICO opens, they will provide an address, and you can send Ether to that address.

Tokens in an ICO are usually limited, and when all the tokens are sold, the ICO is complete. This often results in many transactions at the start of ICO, causing delays in the transaction times.

Gas Price and Gas Limit

Applications to an ICO are treated like transactions to a smart contract. They are processed by miners that receive a fee for processing the transaction.

Gas Price and Gas Limit determine the fee the miner receives. The higher the gas price and gas limit you set on a transaction, the faster the transaction will be processed.

During an ICO, the transaction fees paid are much higher, as people want to ensure their transactions are processed faster so they don't miss out if the ICO sells out quickly. The ICO website will usually have a recommended

Gas Limit and Gas Price to send. They may also set a maximum limit to create a fairer offer, ensuring people aren't forced to pay high transaction fees to participate.

If an application is rejected, the transaction fees are still paid, so be careful sending too many transactions or setting the fees above the recommended ICO limit.

Sending bitcoins and other Cryptocurrencies to an ICO

ICOs may allow you to apply by sending bitcoins or other cryptocurrencies.

You can only receive tokens to specific Ethereum addresses and wallets, as mentioned earlier, so if you apply with bitcoins or other cryptocurrencies, make sure you have the correct wallet set up and put that address as the receiving address.

When you send bitcoins or other cryptocurrencies, you can include a note with the transaction. This is the "coinbase" of the transaction. The ICO may specify that you include the receiving address as part of the coinbase of the transaction.

You may also include a refund address if the transaction is rejected. Do not confuse the refund address with the receiving address. A refund address will generally be the address you send the bitcoins or cryptocurrency from. A receiving address is the address where your cryptocurrency tokens will be sent. Mixing these up could result in losing your funds.

Not all cryptocurrency wallets allow you to include a message with a transaction. You may lose your funds if you apply for an ICO with bitcoins, without including a valid Ethereum address that can receive tokens in the coinbase of the transaction.

Receiving tokens

The time to receive tokens in an ICO varies, depending on the ICO. Tokens may not be distributed for months after an ICO completes. When sent, they will be received on the Ethereum address provided. To sell them, you must transfer them to an exchange that accepts the tokens.

Be careful when sending tokens to an exchange address, as you may lose your tokens if you send them to the wrong address.

Final Note on ICOs

A lot of risks are involved in participating in an ICO. Now have an idea of the risks involved and how to avoid many of these risks.

Remember to follow all instructions in the ICO. Take your time to check them carefully and double check all details are correct.

Research an ICO carefully, especially ensuring the ICO is not a scam by reading posts about it on reddit and social media.

Chapter 12: The future of Ethereum

Cryptocurrencies had been around for several years before Ethereum was created. Bitcoin was the first; however, Litecoin, Dogecoin, and other cryptocurrencies had a strong following and community before Ethereum existed.

At the time of writing, Ethereum is only 2 years old compared to Bitcoin, which has been around for 8 years. Ethereum is still in its early days, and its potential is still being realized.

We can only guess what the future of Ethereum holds, given how new it is; however, some trends are emerging, which we can use to predict the potential future of Ethereum.

Enterprise Ethereum Alliance

The formation of the Enterprise Ethereum Alliance led to a significant increase in the price and interest in Ethereum.

The Enterprise Ethereum Alliance has approximately 150 members. These are some of the largest companies in the world, working together to develop the frameworks to use Ethereum within organizations.

This alliance is less than a year old and is still conducting feasibility studies. They have made no major announcements yet about the use of Ethereum in any large global organization.

This alliance has governments and major corporations working together, so it has the potential to make Ethereum a platform used by companies and governments all over the world.

It is also possible, after examining Ethereum, companies and governments decide not to use Ethereum. They may create their own blockchain based systems that don't rely on the Ethereum platform.

Given the number of governments and companies interested in Ethereum, it is a reasonable prediction that Ethereum will be used by major governments and companies. Even if the companies in this alliance decide they won't be using Ethereum, there are thousands of other companies not involved in this alliance looking to utilize Ethereum in their businesses.

Regulation and legislation around ICOs

China recently banned illegal ICOs and cryptocurrency exchanges. There has been little regulation around companies raising funds through ICOs, which has led to scams and investors losing money.

Companies have been using ICOs as a method to raise money, easily avoiding financial and regulatory requirements around raising funds.

People first must convert their fiat currencies into cryptocurrencies before sending those funds to participate in an ICO. People are also not receiving shares in the company but are receiving tokens that can be used in the application when it launches.

These are essentially loopholes that allow companies to get around existing legislation. As companies are receiving funds in cryptocurrencies, not fiat currencies, and people are purchasing tokens, not investing in the company, it is within the law.

Changes to the law lags behind changes to society and technology. There are lengthy investigations, government reports, and court cases before laws are changed. Many governments around the world are looking at ICOs and how to deal with them.

While ICOs are legal in most countries, the ban on ICOs in China may be the future direction other governments take by banning ICOs. If there are no outright bans, there will be increased regulation and requirements for raising funds via an ICO.

Competition from other platforms

Ethereum is revolutionary; however, it’s open source, meaning anyone can get the source code and create their own version. Ethereum Classic is almost identical to Ethereum, and other companies or groups can also create their own version.

Ethereum Classic is much less popular than Ethereum, as blockchain-based systems and cryptocurrencies require a large community that contributes computing power and supports the network. Ethereum has a large network of users with support from businesses and governments.

Ethereum classic likely will not provide much competition to Ethereum; however, China has its own unique blockchain startup space. Platforms, such as NEO, allow developers to create decentralized apps and smart contracts. The majority of computers mining cryptocurrencies are based in China, which provides a large potential community and user base for NEO.

Bitcoin developers may also create a similar platform that uses the Bitcoin network to run dApps and smart contracts. If so, this could pose significant competition for Ethereum and provide an alternative that utilizes Bitcoin for smart contracts and dApps.

The first company to create a new technology is not always the dominant leader in the space after a few years. Ethereum may be the first blockchain based platform to allow the creation of dApps and smart contracts; however, it may not be the dominant platform.

Decentralized Internet

Of all the potential that Ethereum may offer, the most revolutionary may be the ability to replace the structure of the internet with a decentralized internet.

The benefits of decentralized apps and servers was covered earlier in the book. To quickly recap this information, when you access a website, you are accessing it from a central server. All the files, photos, and data you upload are stored on that central server. If that central server is hacked, all data on that central server is vulnerable. If the server goes offline, then the website and all data is also offline.

Ethereum allows websites, applications, and almost anything you can access online today to become decentralized. These websites, apps, and data are stored and accessed from a network of decentralized computers across the world.

This has the potential to replace web hosting companies, file storage companies, and the very structure of the internet. This would create a decentralized internet controlled by individuals, not by large corporations or governments.

Mainstream acceptance

Whether smart contracts, dApps, and the Ethereum platform become more popular depends largely on mainstream acceptance.

Most people don't care about terms like "decentralization" or "censor-proof." They are more concerned with terms such as "security." There may not be a need for most people to use dApps or smart contracts, and the benefits are not appealing compared to existing options.

Removing third-party intermediaries is not a benefit to many people, as it means there is no customer service to contact or physical location they can go to. While all people may agree they don't like being put on hold when calling a bank, it is still a better option than having no bank to call.

This is the same problem with all dApps, not just finance related apps. Telling someone to stop using Instagram and use a different photo app because it's decentralized is hardly a compelling argument for most selfie-loving users of Instagram.

If companies can create dApps that appeal to a mainstream market, then people may use Ethereum because they want to use those dApps. If there are no dApps that people want to use or compelling enough reasons to use it, then they are unlikely to gain popularity or replace current options.

If people can earn cryptocurrencies by using a photo sharing dApp, this could be a compelling reason to use a dApp. Celebrity acceptance of dApps could also be a reason people use dApps; however, celebrity acceptance is more likely to be linked to earning money than benefits such as decentralization.

End of Chapter Notes on the Future of Ethereum

The future of Ethereum is still uncertain. Whether governments and major companies replace existing systems with an Ethereum based solution is still unknown.

Ethereum is still new, and the applications created on it are very basic. When the internet first launched, most websites were little more than text and some links. It was many years before websites became as advanced as they are today.

The capabilities of Ethereum may pale in comparison to the future possibilities. Today’s dApps are comparable to the basic text only websites when the internet first launched. At the moment, we can only imagine what the future of Ethereum holds. Given the rate that technology rapidly advances, it may surpass our wildest predictions.

CPSIA information can be obtained
at www.ICGtesting.com
Printed in the USA
LVHW062209270122
709439LV00005B/252

9 781804 319666